To Brian, my husband and dance partner
—A. D. P.

To my buddies James and Floyd
—B. P.

ALVIN AILEY

Andrea Davis Pinkney

Illustrated by

Brian Pinkney

Hyperion Paperbacks for Children
New York

Acknowledgments

It is with deep gratitude that the author and illustrator thank the following people for sharing their memories about Alvin Ailey's life and for offering their support to this project:

Mrs. Lula Elizabeth Cooper, Alvin Ailey's mother, who told colorful stories about Alvin's boyhood

Laura Beaumont, director, marketing and public relations, Alvin Ailey American Dance Theater

Mickey Bord, archivist, Alvin Ailey American Dance Theater

Carmen de Lavallade, guest artist, Alvin Ailey American Dance Theater

Audrey Edwards, editor at large, *Essence* magazine

Robyn Govan, mentor and friend to the author

Ella Thompson Moore, former dancer, Alvin Ailey American Dance Theater; artistic director, Charles Moore Dance Theatre

Stephanie Stokes Oliver, editor, *Essence* magazine

Dorene Richardson, former dancer, Alvin Ailey American Dance Theater

James Truitte, former principal dancer, Alvin Ailey American Dance Theater; professor of dance, University of Cincinnati, College Conservatory of Music

Sylvia Waters, artistic director, Alvin Ailey Repertory Ensemble

Valerie Wilson Wesley, executive editor, *Essence* magazine

The author would also like to acknowledge Jacqueline Quinn Moore Latham for her biographical study on the life and contributions of Alvin Ailey.

Author's Note

Alvin Ailey is a biographical narrative history based on actual events that occurred during Alvin Ailey's lifetime. The individuals, places, dates, and dance numbers cited throughout are real. Dialogue has been created to weave the story together.

First Hyperion Paperback edition 1995

Text © 1993 by Andrea Davis Pinkney.
Illustrations © 1993 by Brian Pinkney.

All rights reserved. For information address Hyperion Books for Children,
114 Fifth Avenue, New York, New York 10011-5690.

Printed in Singapore by Tien Wah Press Pte Ltd

11 12 13 14 15 16 17 18 19 20

The artwork for this book is prepared as scratchboard renderings, hand-colored with oil pastels.
This book is set in 16-point Cochin.

Library of Congress Cataloging-in-Publication Data
Pinkney, Andrea Davis.
Alvin Ailey/Andrea Davis Pinkney: illustrated by Brian Pinkney—
1st ed.   p.   cm.
Summary: Describes the life, dancing, and choreography of Alvin Ailey, who created his
own modern dance company to explore the black experience.
ISBN 1-56282-413-9 (trade) — ISBN 1-56282-414-7 (lib. bdg.) — ISBN 0-7868-1077-7 (pbk.)
1. Ailey, Alvin—Juvenile literature. 2. Dancers—United States—
Biography—Juvenile literature. [1. Ailey, Alvin. 2. Dancers.
3. Choreography. 4. Afro-Americans—Biography.] I. Pinkney, J. Brian, ill. II. Title.
GV1785.A38P56   1993   792.8'028'092—dc20   92-54865

1942

True Vine Baptist Church

It seemed like the hottest day ever in Navasota, Texas, the small, dusty town where Alvin Ailey and his mother, Lula, lived. Blue-black flies buzzed their songs while the church bell rang.

Alvin and Lula worshiped at True Vine Baptist Church every Sunday. When they arrived for services, Alvin slid into his usual seat in the first-row pew. There he could watch his mother sing in the gospel choir. And Lula sure could sing. Her voice rose clear and strong as she sang the morning hymn.

The men at True Vine dressed in dignified suits. The women showed off wide-brimmed hats and fanned away the Texas heat. Some cuddled powdered babies; others hugged their Bibles.

True Vine's Reverend Lewis delivered a thundering sermon. The organ rang out, followed by a bellow of tenors singing "Rocka My Soul in the Bosom of Abraham."

Sweet sopranos and tambourines joined the rousing refrain:

Rocka-my-soul in the bosom of Abraham
Rocka-my-soul in the bosom of Abraham
Rocka-my-soul in the bosom of Abraham
Ohhh, rocka-my-soul....

The congregation made a joyful noise. They stepped and swayed with the warmth of the spirit and raised their palms in revelation. Alvin stomped his feet and clapped his hands so hard, they hurt. "Ohhh... rocka-my-soul...," he sang along.

Alvin was going to miss the music and rejoicing at True Vine Baptist Church.

Days later, Alvin rode a creaky locomotive headed west. He and Lula were going to try life in Los Angeles, California. Times had been hard in Texas; there weren't many jobs. Lula wanted a better life for Alvin. She told him there were more opportunities in the city, more ways to make a decent living.

Alvin stared out his window while the train rocked and lurched its way through the dry Texas land. Life in the city would be so different.

1945–1947
Los Angeles

Los Angeles was a flashy town. Lula found plenty of work. Most mornings she left their apartment on East 43rd Place before sunrise, and she didn't return home until the sun was long past setting.

Alvin didn't mind, though. On Saturdays and after school he liked spending time alone, exploring the city streets. He strolled Central Avenue, where nightclubs such as the Club Alabam boomed with the sounds of big-band jazz—swinging music that spilled out into the street—while the musicians inside rehearsed for the evening show.

Alvin especially liked downtown Los Angeles, where the lights on the theater houses reflected off the pavement. There was the Orpheum Theater, the Biltmore, the Rosebud, and the Lincoln.

Outside each theater a blinking marquee announced the latest show:

Pearl Bailey Performing Live
Billie Holiday — A Night of Blues
Duke Ellington and His Band

The men who owned the theaters stacked handbills on their stoops. Each handbill announced coming attractions. Alvin collected them all.

He dawdled along the sidewalk and spotted a handbill showing a black dancer, something Alvin had never seen advertised before. The paper said

Coming Soon to the Biltmore Theater
Katherine Dunham and Her Dancers
in
Tropical Revue

Alvin looked carefully at the picture of Katherine Dunham, a beautiful dancer fluttering exotic ruffles. Katherine Dunham and her dance troupe were one of the few traveling shows in the world with black dancers performing dances from Africa, Haiti, and Latin America.

Alvin was curious. As he tucked the announcement into his pocket, he noticed Ted Crumb, a skinny boy with spindly legs, hanging out at a stage door nearby.

Ted knew all kinds of things about dance; he hoped to dance onstage someday. Ted told Alvin that Katherine Dunham's afternoon show was about to start and that they could see dancing like they'd never seen before.

Alvin and Ted crept down the alley that led to the Biltmore's stage entrance. They kept quiet and out of sight. With the stage door opened just so, they watched the splendor of *Tropical Revue*.

Katherine Dunham and her dancers swirled and lunged to the rhythms of West Indian drums. They were famous for *Bahiana,* a spicy Brazilian routine, and for a sizzling number called *Rumba with a Little Jive Mixed In.* Alvin's soul danced along when he saw Katherine Dunham's style.

Alvin nudged Ted. "What is that they're doing? What *is* that?" he asked.

"That's modern dancing," Ted said. "Watch this!"

Ted tried Katherine Dunham's *Bahiana*. Alvin slapped out a beat on his knees and followed Ted's lead.

Slowly, Alvin began to move. He curled his shoulders from back to front and rippled his hands like an ocean wave. He rolled his hips in an easy, steady swivel, dancing with an expression all his own.

Alvin moved like a cat, *smooth* like quicksilver. When he danced, happiness glowed warm inside him.

Dusk crept over the city. The streetlights of Central Avenue winked on, one by one. Alvin made his way back to East 43rd Place.

That night, Alvin told his mother he'd seen black people performing their own special dances. It was a show Alvin would never forget.

1949–1953
Lester Horton's Dance School

More than anything, Alvin wanted to study dance. But when Alvin arrived in Los Angeles not everyone could take dance lessons. In 1949 not many dance schools accepted black students. And almost none taught the fluid moves that Alvin liked so much — almost none but the Lester Horton Dance Theater School, a modern dance school that welcomed students of all races.

Lester's door was open to anyone serious about learning to dance. And, at age eighteen, Alvin Ailey was serious, especially when he saw how Lester's dancers moved. One student, Carmen de Lavallade, danced with a butterfly's grace. Another, James Truitte, made modern dance look easy. But Lester worked his students hard. Sometimes they danced all day.

After hours in the studio, droplets of sweat dotted Alvin's forehead. He tingled inside, ready to try Lester's steps once more. At first, Alvin kept time to Lester's beat and followed Lester's moves. Then Alvin's own rhythm took over, and he started creating his own steps. Alvin's tempo worked from his belly to his elbows, then oozed through his thighs and feet.

"What is Alvin *doing*?" one student asked.

"Whatever he's doing, he's sure doing it fine," two dancers agreed.

Some tried to follow Alvin's moves, but even Alvin didn't know which way his body would reel him next.

Alvin's steps flowed from one to another. His loops and spins just came to him, the way daydreams do.

Alvin danced at Lester Horton's school almost every day. He taught the other students his special moves.

In 1950, Alvin joined Lester Horton's dance company. Soon Alvin performed his own choreography for small audiences who gathered at Lester's studio. Alvin's dances told stories. He flung his arms and shim-shammed his middle to express jubilation. His dips and slides could even show anger and pain. Modern dance let Alvin's imagination whirl.

All the while, Lester watched Alvin grow into a strong dancer and choreographer. Lester told Alvin to study and learn as much as he could about dance. He encouraged Alvin to use his memories and his African-American heritage to make dances that were unforgettable.

1958–1960
Blues Suite–Revelations

Alvin's satchel hung heavy on his shoulder. His shoes rapped a beat on the sidewalk while taxicabs honked their horns. He was glad to be in New York City, where he came to learn ballet from Karel Shook and modern dance techniques from Martha Graham, two of the best teachers in the world.

Alvin took dance classes all over town, and he met dancers who showed him moves he'd never seen before. So many dancers were black. Like Alvin, their dreams soared higher than New York's tallest skyscrapers.

Alvin gathered some of the dancers he'd seen in classes around the city. He chose the men and women who had just the right moves to dance his choreography. Alvin told them he wanted to start a modern dance company that would dance to blues and gospel music — the heritage of African-American people. Nine dancers believed in Alvin's idea. This was the beginning of the Alvin Ailey American Dance Theater.

On March 30, 1958, on an old wooden stage at the 92nd Street Y, Alvin and his friends premiered with *Blues Suite*, dances set in a honky-tonk dance hall. Stage lights cast moody shadows against the glimmer of each dancer's skin. The women flaunted red-hot dresses with shoes and stockings to match; the men wore black hats slouched low on their heads. They danced to the swanky-swank of a jazz rhapsody.

Alvin's choreography depicted the blues, that weepy sadness all folks feel now and then. *Blues Suite* stirred every soul in the room.

Alvin was on his way to making it big. Word spread quickly about him and his dancers. Newspapers hailed Alvin. Radio stations announced his debut.

An even bigger thrill came when the 92nd Street Y asked Alvin to perform again. He knew they hardly ever invited dance companies to come back. Alvin was eager to show off his next work.

On January 31, 1960, gospel harmonies filled the concert hall at the 92nd Street Y.

Rock-rock-rock
Rocka-my-soul
Ohhh, rocka-my-soul

Alvin clapped in time to the music, the same way he did when he was a boy. But now, Alvin rejoiced onstage in *Revelations*, a suite of dances he created to celebrate the traditions of True Vine Baptist Church in Navasota, Texas.

The audience swayed in their seats as Alvin and his company gloried in their dance. High-stepping ladies appeared onstage sweeping their skirts. They danced with grace and haughty attitudes. Alvin and the other men jumped lively to the rhythm, strutting and dipping in sassy revelry.

Revelations honored the heart and the dignity of black people while showing that hope and joy are for everyone. With his sleek moves, Alvin shared his experiences and his dreams in a way no dancer had ever done.

When *Revelations* ended, the audience went wild with applause. They stomped and shouted. "More!" they yelled. *"More!"*

Taking a bow, Alvin let out a breath. He raised his eyes toward heaven, satisfied and proud.

By exploring the African-American cultural experience through dance, Alvin Ailey changed the face of American dance forever. The Alvin Ailey American Dance Theater (AAADT) was one of the first integrated American dance companies to gain international fame. Two years after the creation of *Revelations*, Mr. Ailey's company performed in the Far East, Southeast Asia, and Australia on a tour sponsored by the U.S. State Department. Since Mr. Ailey founded his company in 1958, it has performed for an estimated 15 million people in forty-eight states, forty-five countries, and on six continents.

In 1965, Mr. Ailey met Judith Jamison, a vibrant young dancer whose talent and energy inspired him to create *Cry*, a piece that honors the struggles and triumphs of black women. That 1971 work is now a popular Alvin Ailey classic.

Mr. Ailey was born in Rogers, Texas, on January 5, 1931. During his life, Mr. Ailey received many honors. In 1982, he received the United Nations Peace Medal. He was awarded the Kennedy Center Honor and the Handel Medallion in December 1988. Mr. Ailey died on December 1, 1989, in New York City.

Today, under the direction of Ms. Jamison, the Alvin Ailey American Dance Theater still mesmerizes audiences everywhere. Mr. Ailey's dance tradition continues at the Alvin Ailey American Dance Center—an accredited dance academy in New York City—where boys and girls study ballet, modern dance, and tap dance. The Alvin Ailey Repertory Ensemble, the resident company of the school, is a troupe of young dancers who perform throughout the United States.